T0195917

FOR THE
LOVE OF
THE LORD

PART 1 TO BE CONTINUED......

-A TRUE STORY OF TWO PEOPLE MIRACULOUSLY
BROUGHT TOGETHER BY THE LORD WITH
SIGNS AND WONDERS-

JEREMIAH MARK GUTHRIE

WESTBOW
P R E S S®
A DIVISION OF THOMAS NELSON
& ZONDERVAN

WestBow Press books may be ordered through booksellers or by contacting:

WestBow Press
A Division of Thomas Nelson & Zondervan
1663 Liberty Drive
Bloomington, IN 47403
www.westbowpress.com
844-714-3454

Because of the dynamic nature of the Internet, any web addresses or links contained in this book may have changed since publication and may no longer be valid. The views expressed in this work are solely those of the author and do not necessarily reflect the views of the publisher, and the publisher hereby disclaims any responsibility for them.

Any people depicted in stock imagery provided by Getty Images are models, and such images are being used for illustrative purposes only. Certain stock imagery © Getty Images.

ISBN: 979-8-3850-1691-4 (sc)
ISBN: 979-8-3850-1687-7 (e)

Library of Congress Control Number: 2024900804

Print information available on the last page.

WestBow Press rev. date: 01/26/2024

INTRODUCTION

It is April 14, 2023, approximately 1:12 p.m., and I am on a plane headed to Tokyo to meet the woman the Lord has supernaturally revealed to me to be my wife. We met on Facebook on March 22, 2023.

I understand what I write about in this book many may not believe. But I also understand that many will. This book, through the power of the Holy Spirit, will bring glory and honor to our Lord and restore lost faith, hope, and trust in our living God.

This is not a fairy tale, but it sure sounds like one! Just wait and see. And may we venture together on this reading journey that describes God's love toward us and the love he has intentionally allowed a man and a woman to have with each other, making Him the center of their relationship and lighting a fire of revival in their hearts and yours. May it never be put out but preserved by his grace.

Due to some subject matter possibly being hard for the average person to believe, by God's provision and grace, we have included proof, such as time-stamped smart phone pictures, messages, and so on. Also, at the end of each chapter, my new wife Lhynne has included encouraging messages and verses from the Bible. Thank you for your reading and enjoy.

CHAPTER 1

LOOKING BACK

In this first short chapter, please allow me to give you a brief history of the marriage I was in before I met my true love who was sent to me by the Lord. It has to do with the trials and preparations leading up to what this book is all about, which is how the Lord can, did, and does bring two people together in his timing and his will, once we give him a chance, surrender and let go, choose to trust fully in him, and let him lead in faith.

My previous marriage started in April 2014 and lasted until March 21, 2023 (the date the judge officially signed off on the divorce), even though the time of separation was and filing of the dissolution (divorce) was July 2022.

Back in April 2014 when my ex and I got married, I felt we were not in love and had only gone on a few dates. When we went to get married, it was done in secret at night so no one would stop us. No family members or friends were present, just a priest and an unknown witness. I proceeded with the act of marriage (I believe) mostly because I was lonely and impatient for a wife. I had also been drinking before the spontaneous decision to go on the eight-hour drive a couple of states over

(Reno, Nevada) in order to expedite a spontaneous marriage legally.

The marriage (which lasted nine years) from my perspective was quite rocky and seemed to have many more downs than ups. We were not a perfect match or anywhere as we could have been if the Lord had picked our spouses. Nevertheless, we tried to make it work by seeking marriage counseling, but it was to no avail. We were a lot of times barely keeping it together and going through the motions. Our image seemed good to outsiders, but within, we were not as close or intimate as a married couple should be.

I was not perfect; I made mistakes and said the wrong things. She did as well, but toward the end, things occurred that seemed as if they could not be reversed. However, even though things seemed hopeless, I promised the Lord I would try to remain married because it was the right thing to do. Even though I had no more desire left in me to continue, I tried my best once I was able to communicate with her. But by that time, she had already moved on (to my understanding) and made it clear that she was not willing to try any further; she was happy and content, as was my interpretation in our latter communication.

So she proceeded with the divorce filing as the petitioner, and months later, we were finally officially divorced on March 21, 2023.

ENCOURAGING MESSAGES

Yesterday is history, tomorrow is a surprise, and today is a gift from God, which is why we call it the present.

The steadfast love of the Lord never ceases; his mercies never come to an end; they are new every morning, great is your faithfulness. (Lamentations 3:22–23 KJV)

CHAPTER 2

ACCEPTANCE

Several months into the divorce process, I finally got to the point to where I gave up and accepted that it was over, yet I still knew that God could perform a miracle. Perhaps we would divorce but then remarry later, which I was willing to do for the Lord and our son. However, I was apprehensive and scared. I was willing to entertain the idea of us getting back together and reconciling our differences because I desired to honor the Lord regardless of what I felt inside concerning the act of divorce.

I believed at this point that she really was going to proceed with this, and it was going to be official within a matter of weeks at that time, even though it did not actually become official until a few months later. Nevertheless, I started preparing my heart. During that time of preparation, I had gotten on my knees and prayed a special prayer to God about a month or two prior to the divorce being final.

Here is the prayer I prayed to the Lord:

> Dear Lord, I am used to being married, and I want to have a wife too. I do not want to be left high, dry, and lonely. But this time I want you to

bring her to me. She would have to have a heart like mine that genuinely wants to seek after you. She would have to support my music, which is dedicated to preaching the gospel in the future to all ends of the globe. She would need to truly know the Holy Ghost, and she would probably need to be from out of the country, as I have lost trust in the culture of the American woman. Too many things in America are accepted as OK when they are not OK at all—no, not with you, Lord. In Jesus's name. Amen.

This prayer I truly meant in my heart. I did commit to the Lord that I would not engage in dating until after the divorce was final and signed by the judge. I wanted to try to be true to him and do what is right. So about a month and a half later, I got an email from my attorney saying that the judge had signed off on the divorce, but I did not look at the date of the signature. This has much meaning later in this book!

ENCOURAGING MESSAGES

Accepting the situation we have is like surrendering to the Lord and trusting in his way, his plan.

God reminds us of this power and gives us difficulties to bring out the best in us. His promise in his Word offers peace to our hearts in hard situations. It was written in his excellent, powerful book the Holy Bible for his people when times were difficult.

It gives us great hope in the battles we face today, like rays of light breaking through the darkest night.

Yea, though I walk through the valley of the shadow of death, I will fear no evil: for thou art with me; thy rod and thy staff they comfort me. (Psalm 23:4 KJV)

CHAPTER 3

STARTING TO DATE

As soon as I got word that the judge had finally signed off on the divorce, I wasted no time to start the dating process. The first thing to do was to activate a Facebook dating profile. I'd had one without a picture shortly before that, as I was curious about what was out there for viewing and observation purposes. So now that the divorce was final and I was free to date, I activated it with a picture for my profile. I looked at probably one hundred women; almost all of them I did not like, and most of them were unattractive to me. And if they were slightly attractive, the profile was unattractive to me when reading it. It was discouraging and disheartening.

At the minimum, I insisted on finding a true Christian, not just a faker, and I desired to be celibate until we were married. These factors would disqualify me for many women on there from what I perceived. I just wanted something real and true, and I wanted it to last this time. I wanted it to be the last time I got married. I never wanted to go through a divorce again.

On the first day of my profile being active, I received a Facebook friend request (not a dating friend request) from some strange, beautiful woman I did not know. She had sent a request before, but I had ignored her because her profile picture seemed attractive, and I was still technically married at the time. Even though the divorce was sure, it was still not right to me in the Lord's style, standards, and ways. The woman who had friend requested me was unaware that I was married, as she had seen my profile pop up and had sent the request out of sheer curiosity, not with intentions to date.

Nevertheless, I finally accepted her friend request because the divorce was now final. But little did I realize that the divorce had only been signed the day prior, rather than maybe a week ago as I had assumed. My attorneys were slow to get back to me with news.

Anyway, little did I know that this mystery woman who I had just clicked on would be my future wife; the Lord himself went out of his way to bring us together. And I mean the Lord did not just go out of his way; he went *way* out of his way! Just to bring us together!

In the coming chapters, you will see why I said in the introduction that many may not believe what is written in this book.

ENCOURAGING MESSAGES

Those who worship God enjoy his protective care—even while they endure difficult situations.

They do not feel alone when they face dire circumstances because they fully surrender to Him and trust His plan.

> He gives them the sure hope of a better future
> when he will undo any harm they currently
> experience. (Psalm 37:29 KJV)

CHAPTER 4

THE FIRST CONTACT

So as I stated, I accepted this mystery woman's friend request and decided to click on her profile. As I studied her profile, I quickly noticed she was abnormally beautiful. I was slightly discouraged by this because, in America, based on my past observations and experience, the prettier they are, the more likely they are to treat men badly. I suppose this could apply to both men and women.

I read some of her posts and after only a few minutes, it felt as if my heart leaped. I could hardly believe what I was reading; many of her posts were about the Lord, loving and forgiving people, the Bible, the spirit of God, worship songs, and so on.

To me, this was so incredibly rare. I absolutely had to send her a message; I had no choice. So, I sent her a message that said, "Who are you? How did you find me? You appear to have a heart like mine, and this is way out of my character for me, just messaging you like this, because I am normally quite shy."

She is quite shy too. She responded, and that was the first day of the rest of our lives together. A new beginning with the Lord.

Feeling his power and presence, his manifested miracles,

and the other amazing things that I felt led me to share my journey with the world. I want this book to restore hope to the broken-hearted, the single people who feel alone, the people who have ever wondered if God listens or cares, the people who often wonder if they are going to be alone for the rest of their lives, and the people who are thinking about compromising or settling. Wait for him, trust in him, and seek him. Give the Lord a chance and put your trust and faith in what his holy Word says.

Soon we were messaging each other several times a day, in awe and almost disbelief at what the other one was saying. Finally, we started FaceTiming and calling each other every day. Our calls always ended with spirit-filled prayer. Some calls lasted over five hours. It was a mere twenty-three days after our first contact on messenger that I was on a plane from the USA to Tokyo with a ring that I planned to give to her on the top of a famous mountain in Japan called Mount Takao.

What happened during and after those twenty-three days was absolutely amazing, and I will discuss those events further later in this book. But I will write this as a testimony and account of events that took place at the very minimum. We have documented proof: pictures that are time stamped, a video, and dated messages. But first I will tell you about the amazing things that we discovered about each other and have in common. To me, this goes to show just how perfect our God is. He really, truly knows what he is doing when it comes to a man and a woman who are destined by and through him to be together as husband and wife. The Lord makes no mistakes.

Also, I would like to point out how and why she even found me on Facebook in the first place. Even after our messages and calls, I was still so curious as to how and why she even found me, seeing as she was living in Japan and I in the US at the time. No, it was not on a Facebook dating site. What I found out was that apparently my profile had popped up on her Facebook page as a suggested friend. So she had glanced at my profile photo because she thought that I was handsome and my baby son, who I was holding in the picture, was very cute. She had also thought that I appeared to be a loving dad. She had been amazed by the photo. Nevertheless, she'd passed over my profile and proceeded to look at the others that had popped up as well. She'd thought she would never see my profile again.

However, the Lord our God had other plans. Later that same day, she got on Facebook and noticed that my profile had shown up again! Yes, a second time on the very same day. She had thought that to be strange as she had never noticed a stranger's profile popping up on her Facebook two times in one day before. Regardless, she passed over it again, and she again assumed she would never see my profile again. But get this! Later that same day (yes, the same day still), my profile showed up again for a third time! This time, she could not ignore it, and she, just out of sheer curiosity, sent me a friend request. She asked herself, "What is this, Lord?" Also, she did not even read or view my profile but only sent me a friend request.

In her mind, I looked too young. She was interested in guys who were older than her. She would never accept or consider dating someone who was younger than her, not in a million years. She was strict about that, and most of her friends and family knew that about her as well. She was forty-five and I was forty-two at that time, which happened to still be our ages when I wrote this chapter. So truly, the only reason she sent me the friend request was because my profile had popped up three times in just that one day.

ENCOURAGING MESSAGES

Psalm 37:5–6 encourages us to delight ourselves in the Lord and commit everything we do to the Lord, trusting that he will help us. To achieve success, we must give our plans to the Lord. God gives us difficulties to bring out the best in us. God does not give you the people you want; he gives you the people you need. He gives you the people you need to help you, to hurt you, to leave you, to love you, and to make you the person you are meant to be.

CHAPTER 5

THINGS WE HAVE IN COMMON

Even though having things in common does not constitute a miracle or a divine appointment or hookup with your soulmate, it can still set the stage for God's romantic display of his love toward us. He shows us how much he cares about us and how much he is in control by further confirming that this person could be our soulmate. His spirit dwells inside of us and is all around us, in control of all things.

As we began to communicate through Facebook messages, one of the first things we noticed that we have in common is our birthdays, which are only ten days apart. Hers is on September 20, and mine is on September 30.

Also, we have both had a prior experience casting a demon out of a possessed person by the power of the Holy Ghost and in the name of Jesus. It had been my first experience dealing with such a thing, and the idea of finding anybody with a similar experience seemed incredibly unlikely. Because of that, we started to take each other more seriously than we normally would have. When she found out I had gone through a similar situation, it made her cry.

Also, we have both been persecuted by people in the church and falsely accused by our own church members in the past.

One of the most meaningful things to me that we both share is that she has spoken in tongues and has been baptized by the Holy Spirit. We share the same type of heart, which became incredibly obvious to both of us as we developed our fast-growing relationship. The presence of the Lord almost always makes me weep, but few other things ever seem to affect me like that, as it is much harder for a man to cry than it is a woman, according to my observations in life. The presence of the Lord always affects her in that way as well.

Our desires are the same. We both deeply desire God to be number one in our relationship and to grow closer and closer to him because we understand that without him as number one, our relationship, as well as any other relationship, is bound to fail. We both gave up, surrendered, and asked God to bring us the one. I tried, but in my heart, I had given up. Deep down, I knew there was no point in dating without the Lord's intervention as I did not want to go through another failed marriage ever again. She felt the same way.

Shockingly, we both take scissors and cut most of our shirts to make them V-necks if they are not already. I have been doing that for about twenty-five years, and she has also for around that long. Personally, I have never encountered anybody else who does that with their shirts in all my life except for my late father, who passed away over twenty years ago. She was quite shocked by this too. I do not know who was more surprised about the shirt cutting. It is such a strange thing to have in common.

Also, before I forget, we are both left-handed. We did not find that out until the first time I visited her in Tokyo. We both have the gift of grace from the Lord, meaning we are both quick to forgive those who hurt us rather than holding onto grudges. I thank the Lord that he has molded us to be this way throughout the years. I cherish and value that quality and rely on the Lord to maintain that in us, as it is not of us but from him and his workings inside of our hearts that we share this attribute.

Another quality I like that we both have in common is we both have strong faith and conviction that anything is possible. We believe in the healing of the sick and the raising of the dead by the power of the Holy Spirit in the name of Jesus Christ, Yeshua, our Lord and Savior. We believe in what the Holy Bible says, which is the living Word of God. Every word in it is true and alive, and we can take any scripture that exists in his Word on faith.

Our favorite color is blue. She had prayed for a Caucasian guy with blue eyes most of her life, and I am a Caucasian guy with blue eyes. We both love spicy foods as well as all the same foods really. We both prefer to be alone rather than out in public or in crowds. We are both very shy typically. We are both imperfect, especially me.

Did I say especially me? Oh, yes, I did. OK, well, allow me to say that about a hundred, maybe a thousand times more! But that would probably make this book too long, so I will just skip over that and go back to what I was writing about.

Most importantly, we both have a deep love, or passion, in our hearts for the Lord, despite our imperfections.

One of my favorite things we have in common is our love for playing Christian or worship music. For years, I have played Christian or worship music twenty-four hours a day nonstop in my home (except when not living by myself). The same with her! I even asked her a few times to specify her meaning of "24-7, nonstop." Even at night when you sleep? Yes! Both of us doing the same again! And there are many, many more things that we amazingly have in common with each other!

ENCOURAGING MESSAGES

God's plan is always the best, and sometimes the process can be painful and hard. However, it's important to remember that when God is silent, he is doing something good for you, for me, and for us. We must remember the importance of believing in God and acting in faith to see victory in our lives. God's plan for each and every one of us is always bigger, bolder, filled with a lot of surprises, and better than anything we could ever imagine. He is faithful.

> For I know the thoughts that I think towards you, saith the Lord, thoughts of peace, and not of evil, to give you an expected end. (Jeremiah 29:11 KJV)

> God is not a man, that he should lie; neither the son of man, that he should repent: hath he said, and shall he not do it? or hath he spoken, and shall he not make it good? (Numbers 23:19 KJV)

CHAPTER 6

SHOW ME THE RAINBOW

As I promised, this chapter contains one of the biggest supernatural signs we had experienced together up to this point in our relationship, which is before I flew to Tokyo to see her. (I will talk more about the amazing experience Lyhnne and I had in Tokyo later.) Lhynne asked me in a message if I would do her a favor and please help her pray for the Lord to show her a rainbow in the next three to five days. I was confused by this. I did not know how to respond because I did not know what she meant and was hesitant to ask her. My only response was OK. In my mind, I thought it was some Japanese saying, perhaps meaning "let me see the light" in order to come to some sort of understanding about a certain situation or decision. Little did I know that she actually quite literally and specifically wanted the Lord to send her a real, actual rainbow as a sign that we are meant to be and that I am the man chosen for her to marry. Not only that but this rainbow needed to come in the next three to five days.

Two days later, I was building a privacy fence in my backyard when I decided to walk out to the truck that was parked in my driveway. Upon doing so, I looked up and saw the most beautiful rainbow. This was the second rainbow that God sent, as the first rainbow (which I will explain in more detail in the following paragraph) appeared in nearly the same spot two days prior, only hours after Lhynne's prayer. I decided to take a video and a couple of photos of it like I usually do when I see a nice rainbow.

Shortly after, thinking nothing of what Lhynne had asked for two days prior, I decided to send her the video and a couple of the pictures. In fact, I almost decided not to, but I went ahead and did so anyway because I thought she might like it. Soon afterward, she messaged me and then called me crying and crying in disbelief. That was the sign she had asked for. But she said the Lord chose to show it to me first, referring to the man as the head and spiritual leader of the household. Just like when Moses went to the mountain to seek God and, when done, revealed to the people what the Lord had said to him.

Once I realized what had happened and remembered her message to me two days prior, I, too, was blown away. That meant so much to her that she marked the dates of that event— March 30 and April 1—as if to celebrate them as a holiday every year from then on. Now regarding the first rainbow; on March 30, 2023, at 2:23 a.m., she sent me a message asking me to "help her pray for the rainbow."

Well, the very same day at 6:59 p.m., I had walked out to my truck and saw a beautiful single rainbow. I then took one video and a few pictures of it like I usually do when I see a rainbow. Afterward, I had thought nothing of it. I did not send the picture or the video to her and most likely never would have. The pictures and video would have been lost in the thousands of pictures I have stored on my smart phone.

Then on April 1, 2023, at 5:43 p.m., another rainbow appeared, this time a double rainbow and much brighter. As

I stated earlier, I took videos and pictures. But this time I sent them to Lhynne, which is why I think the Lord sent this second rainbow, because I did not send her any pictures of the first one or even as much as tell her about it. I'd totally forgotten that she had sent me her prayer request about a rainbow as a sign. In this book, I will include a photo of both rainbows with time stamps on the pictures as well as a photo of the message she sent me, time-stamped as well. Tokyo is thirteen hours ahead of the US in the spring. Either way, the second rainbow came exactly two days after her message to me, her prayer, and the first rainbow that I ignored.

In addition to this miracle, I would like to include another sign that was given to us around a week prior to the rainbow from God. Since we first met on Facebook messenger, Lhynne would take a picture of the front page of her daily devotional and send it to me almost every day. I remember always admiring it and the wording, thinking how much I would like to have a daily devotional like hers. I wondered where in Japan she had purchased it. I even told her how much I liked her devotional. I was, in a way, a little jealous, I think.

A couple of weeks after that, I was in my shop going through a basket of some of my belongings and books. I noticed this old-looking, small book made from some sort of leatherlike material. It was falling apart. Out of curiosity, I decided to open it up and noticed it was a devotional! But upon further inspection, I suddenly realized it was not just any daily devotional, it was the exact same devotional Lhynne had; it was by the exact same author with the exact same wording on the exact same days with the exact same daily scriptures! It was just a much older copy than hers. I was totally blown away and felt like I could hardly believe that I actually had the same book already. I even called up my mom to ask if she had ever given me that book, and I tried hard to remember exactly where that book came from, why I had it, and who had given it to me.

I immediately took a picture of it and sent it to Lhynne and told her what had just happened; we exchanged pictures of each other's devotionals, verifying that, yes, they were the same! This made Lhynne cry tears of joy and amazement. It was yet another confirmation to us out of many that God is with us and we are meant to be.

Now back to the rainbow! To me, that was God answering Lhynne's prayer the very same day but me ignoring it, or not remembering her prayer request, so two days later, the Lord sent another one in the exact same spot in the sky, only this time much brighter and doubled, trying to get my attention. I finally sent Lhynne the pictures and video of the second much brighter answer to her prayer.

ENCOURAGING MESSAGES

Faith can move the mountain!

Faith is the assurance of things hoped for, everything not seen. With faith as small as a mustard seed, there is no mountain, no obstacle, and no hindrance in our lives that we cannot overcome. Faith is powerful. With faith, nothing is impossible for us. With God on our side, there is no mountain in our lives that we cannot move with our faith.

> Faith changes everything. As believers in Christ, we walk by faith, not by sight. (2 Corinthians 5:7 KJV)

CHAPTER 7

ARRIVING IN TOKYO

In the introduction to this book, I was on a plane headed to Tokyo, Japan, to see the love of my life in person for the very first time. Well, let's fast forward to my arrival!

It was a long flight. But it gave me around eleven hours to write most of the rough draft of this book. As I exited the plane, since I was a foreigner, I had to go through an extensive security check typically referred to as customs. Usually, in customs, there is a really long line of other foreign travelers who must go through the same process before the airport officials will allow any of them to step foot outside of the airport. This was an intimidating and stressful experience for me as this was my first time ever traveling to another country.

The line was very long and slow, and I believe it took around three hours in multiple lines before I was finally free to leave the airport. During that time, Lhynne and I were able to communicate with our cell phones. We were both so excited when the plane landed, and the excitement and anticipation of soon meeting each other was hard to handle due to the extensive customs process.

Nevertheless, the moment when we made contact finally

came. My back was turned, and I heard this beautiful, excited voice calling my name over and over. I turned around as she ran up to me, nearly in tears, and hugged me as we stood just outside one of the airport exits.

As we were hugging each other, we could feel the presence of the Lord strongly loom over us, further reassuring our hearts this truly was a divine appointment from the Lord. We finally ended our hug and held each other's hands. While walking to her friend Jenny's car, I could feel something that I have never felt so strongly before in all of my life. I could feel what I believe now was the love of our Lord Jesus coming from within her heart, through her hand, and into me. It was love but more so in a physical form rather than an emotional one. I could discern her heart while holding her hand, and I could somehow feel that this woman genuinely and truly loved me so much with a love that was so pure. This feeling had such an impact on me that even months later, whenever I thought about that moment, I would feel that same feeling all over again.

My stay in Tokyo was only for four days, and during my visit, our time together was so amazing and special. One of the biggest miracles I have ever had happen to me in all of my life occurred during this time together with Lhynne up on top of Mount Takao in Tokyo, Japan.

In the next chapter, I am going to write about a truly remarkable experience, and if I did not have proof, I don't know how many people would actually believe what happened. But our faithful and perfect Lord Jesus, he knew already that it would be hard for the world to believe without proof, so he provided us with the necessary pictures and evidence to show to the world that, yes, this is true! Yes, this is real! Yes, this really did actually happen!

So hold on to your seats, brace yourselves, and enjoy as

you continue to read, and may this testimony you are about to experience remove the veil of doubt you may have been holding onto in your life. May it ignite the fire of hope in your heart toward God, which may have once been lost within you. May it restore your faith that there really is a God, and he really does care about you and loves us, that he really does hear our prayers and really is listening. May it lead you to realize, or perhaps remind you, that God truly is divine, he truly is in control of all things, and nothing can slip past him. All things, all events, all creation, and all that exists is truly in his hands.

ENCOURAGING MESSAGES

Yes, yes, yes! God answers our prayers.

He listens to all of our prayers, regardless of what we ask, and he promises to listen and respond. His answer may be some variation of no, yes, wait, or not now. If he gives us what we ask for, it's because of his great love for us. But if he doesn't give us what we ask for, he's protecting us from it.

> And whatsoever ye shall ask in my name, that will I do, that the Father may be glorified in the Son. (John 14:13 KJV)

CHAPTER 8

THE RING

As I mentioned earlier, during my stay in Tokyo, Japan, visiting Lhynne, one of the big events we had planned was to hike to the top of Mount Takao. Once we reached the top, we planned to eat lunch and then find a spot to pray together. We had planned this several weeks before my visit, and Lhynne was optimistic that the Lord would speak to us there and that he had a surprise for us during that special and sacred moment. What she didn't know was that I had come to Tokyo with an engagement ring and planned to give it to her when we reached the top of the mountain.

Please allow me to go back to a few weeks before this day, to before I had left the United States for Tokyo. I had asked the Lord in prayer if I could get Lhynne an engagement ring and present it to her in Tokyo to ask her to marry me. It quickly became obvious to me that the answer was definitely a yes. So I'd said, "Dear Lord, I am going to shop for a ring, but I really don't know what Japanese women like as far as what style, stone, cut, and so on. I am not familiar with Japanese culture. I ask of you that you pick it out for me. Please make sure that it is a ring that she will really like. Thank you, Lord. I trust that you will pick out the right one for me." I did not write down my prayer at the time, but this is close to the exact wording I used. The point is that I specifically asked the Lord to pick out the ring for me. (Lhynne is part Japanese, part Filipina, and part Spanish, but has lived in Japan for over thirty years.)

After I had prayed, I wasted no time looking at rings on my smart phone. I probably looked at one hundred rings at least that were for sale locally, and even some in another state hundreds of miles away. However, very early on in my search I had seen this one ring and had immediately been drawn to it, and throughout my search, I kept going back to it, admiring it because of how beautiful and unique a ring I thought it was. Eventually, I spoke to the Lord. "Dear Lord, I intend to buy this ring. If this is not the one, please stop me or speak to my heart to tell me not to buy it. Otherwise, I plan on buying it, because I feel this is the one."

So, a couple days later, I went to my appointment I had made with the owner of the ring. I purchased the ring as is and drove home to my house. I did not bother sizing the ring as I had no clue what Lhynne's finger size was. I know what you're thinking: The amazing miracle is that the ring fit! No, that is not the miracle I am referring to in this chapter. Keep reading! It is much more amazing than that, even though, yes, the ring did fit her finger perfectly.

Let's now fast forward to a few weeks later. I am in Japan with the ring in my pocket, getting ready to make the hike to the top of the mountain with my wife-to-be and her friend Jenny, who had been nice enough to drive us around Tokyo during my stay.

There we were, all three of us, at the base of Mount Takao, getting ready to start our amazing, beautiful journey to the summit. It was about a two-hour hike to the top. The date was

April 17, 2023, at around 8:44 a.m. The hike was quite steep at times, and there were many stairs. We stopped many times to rest or take pictures. The hike alone, being able to see the beautiful scenery and amazing Japanese structures, was an experience that I will always treasure and never forget.

We reached the top at around 11:17 a.m. and took many videos and pictures of the famous Mount Fuji since it was clearly visible from the top of Mount Takao. We then decided to rest and prepare to eat the lunch that Lhynne had made for us earlier that morning. After we ate, Lhynne and I decided to seek a place on or near the top of the mountain where we could privately pray together as was our original plan. As we headed slightly down the other side of the mountain, looking for the perfect spot, Lhynne's friend Jenny followed behind us for a while. Just as we started to seek a place, all three of us heard a bird in one of the trees singing this beautiful song. Jenny recognized the song as an old Japanese marriage song of some sort. Both Lhynne and Jenny were amazed by the bird's singing; I thought little of it except that it was a bird making a beautiful whistling sound. I was more content with admiring the excitement of Lhynne and Jenny and their reaction to the bird's singing.

About a half hour later, Lhynne and I found a peaceful spot on the upper side of the mountain that was private and peaceful and looked like the perfect spot for us to pray together. By that point, Jenny had decided to stay behind slightly up the mountain to rest and allow us to be alone together until we were done praying. We sat down on the bench together, which was next to a tree, held hands, and I began to lead us in a prayer, but I was having a hard time praying. I felt in my heart that I needed to propose to her first for some reason.

So I stopped my prayer, reached into my pocket, grabbed

the box that the ring was in, got down on one knee, opened the box, and asked Lhynne to marry me as I presented the ring to her. Thinking nothing of what the size of her finger might be, I took the ring and slid it on her finger. The ring fit perfectly, like it was meant to be but to me, it seemed like it might be just ever so slightly tight. After further observation, I realized that during my excitement, I had put the ring on the wrong finger. I had put it on the right-hand ring finger instead of the left! So, I took it off and switched it to the proper finger and oh my dear Lord! The ring fit so perfectly it was as if it was made custom just for her. It couldn't have fit any more perfectly! Yes, it was 100 percent a *perfect* fit!

She was crying as soon as she saw the ring, before I even asked her to marry me. After she said yes, and upon further observation of the ring, she started crying even more saying, "oh my, oh my! I know this ring; I know this ring!"

Upon hearing her say this, I had no idea what she was talking about but couldn't help but notice that whatever she was talking about was a really big deal to her. Suddenly, she started flipping through picture after picture on her smart phone, desperately looking for something to show me. She wanted so badly to show me a certain picture.

Turns out that on October 2, 2022, (around 6 months before we met) she had taken a picture of an engagement ring she really liked because she had been fantasizing about the Lord bringing her a man to propose to her with a ring like that one someday. In fact, the ring she had taken a picture of came with a matching necklace. She'd bought the necklace but not the ring. Instead, she'd taken a photo of the ring and then prayed to the Lord that he would bring her a man to give her that ring and ask her to marry him. While praying, she knew she had been being wishy-washy and was not actually expecting the Lord to bring her a man with that exact same ring.

Anyway, when she finally found the picture, it was the exact same ring that I had got her! *Yes, yes, yes!* The exact same ring that I had proposed to her with! In this book, I have provided Lyhnne's time-stamped photo of the ring from October 2, 2022, and right next to it, a time-stamped photo of the ring I gave to her, taken on April 14, 2023, right before I flew to Tokyo.

Now get this! About halfway back down the mountain to the car to leave for the day, my mother sent Lhynne and I a text message of a few art photos she had created. One was of a colorful picture of us together which we decided to use in one of our future books, and the other was of a bird and Lhynne. I want to point out that when my mother sent us this photo, she had no idea that Lhynne and I where on Mount Takao, that we had planned to even be on the mountain, or that we had heard a bird in the trees earlier that day whistling a song that meant so much to Lhynne and her friend Jenny. My mother was completely unaware of all of this! So for her to send us those art pictures, and especially the one of the bird, was yet another amazing confirmation from the Lord. This was way too many coincidences, should one try to refer to them as such. But there is a saying: too many coincidences are circumstantial evidence. Yes, in this case, God exists, he is with us, and he is real.

What a way for the Lord to confirm to a couple that they are meant to be together and that their relationship is his plan and from him! And the rainbow too! The diary! All the strange things for two people to have in common, and the timing!

On June 26, 2023, Lyhnne flew from Japan to Oregon, and we got married that very same day! We now live together, ever so happy and blessed and full of thanksgiving and laughter. As I write this and finalize this last chapter, the date is July 17, 2023.

There will be a sequel to this book called *For the Love of the Lord: Part 2*. Also, there will most likely be several more books in my series For the Love of the Lord as this ongoing, real-life love story unfolds. Until then, peace to all.

ENCOURAGING MESSAGES

Hold unto the promise that God is with you in your difficult individual situation. Remember the time in the Bible when God gave Noah a rainbow as a sign that God keeps his promises? As He was faithful to Noah, He will be faithful to you. Generation after generation, trust in him, have faith in him, rely on him, and listen to his instructions.

The promises of God are a source of hope, joy, peace, wisdom, and strength. God has made many promises based on his unwavering love and faithfulness, and the recipients of these promises can have full assurance that what God has pledged will, indeed, be realized. God has also promised new hearts and desires, forgiveness, and a new spirit within us. These promises are the basis for our hope and can be counted on no matter the circumstances or how long the wait.

> Peace I leave with you, my peace I give unto you: not as the world giveth, give I unto you. Let not your heart be troubled, neither let it be afraid. (John 14:27 KJV)

> For the Lord is good; his mercy is everlasting; and his truth endureth to all generations. (Psalm 100:5 KJV)

3-30-23

4-1-23

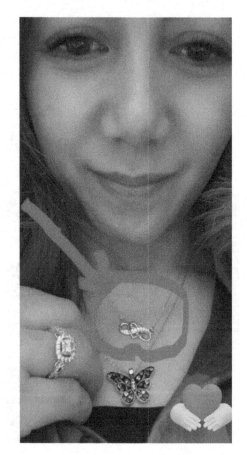

The Matching Necklace

The original picture of the ring with time stamp.

The actual ring I bought her.

Our Wedding Day

Printed in the United States
by Baker & Taylor Publisher Services